SRI HAYAGRIVA STHOTHRAM
Sloka Book

JET Publishing House

INDIA USA

TOWARDS EXCELLENCE

P
R
A
J
N
A

Title	SRI HAYAGRIVA STHOTRAM
Subtitle	Sloka Book
Copyright	Jeeyar Educational Trust
First Edition	2012
Contributor	His Holiness Chinna Jeeyar Swamiji

CONTACT US:

INDIA	UNITED STATES
JIVA Sriramanagaram, Shamshabad, R.R. Dist. Andhra Pradesh - 509 325 Phone: 95535 49971, 95535 499	JETUSA Inc. Jeeyar Asram, 222, Dey Road, CRANBURY, NJ 08512, USA Phone: 609-297-8797

Website: www.prajna4me.org   Email: prajna@jetusa.org

PREFACE

It is difficult to completely explain or even understand the different incarnations of Lord Srimanna:ra:yana, who appeared for the welfare of mankind. Each incarnation has its own significance. Innumerable are the avatha:ras, the appearances of Lord on this earth, for uplifting mankind from miseries.

Lord **S**ri: Ra:ma exemplifies the greatest human qualities like truthfulness & affability. In the avatha:ra of Parasura:ma, he demonstrates the need for the adication of diabolic nature. **S**ri: Va:mana:vatha:ra, on the other hand, shows how Lord supports and protects de:vathas.

Some avatha:ras like Mathsya the divine fish, Vara:ha, the Sacred Boar, Hamsa, the White Swan and Lord Hayagri:va, the divine horse-necked one, appeared to bless humans with knowledge and some showed how that knowledge can be implemented to protect virtues on earth.

Though we are not able to know everything about all these avatha:ras, we must learn about the incarnation of Hayagri:va, which appeared for the distribution of divine knowledge. Let us learn about its significance.

Hayagri:va has His neck like a horse and the body like a human. Just like the Nrusimha:vatha:ra, the form of Hayagri:va is stupendous and surprising. We all know that the ways of God are mysterious, pleasant and wonderful! Sage Ve:da Vya:sa explained about **S**ri: Hayagri:va in 2.7.11 and 5.18.6 of Srimad Bha:gavatha and also in the 11th canto. Even Na:ra:yani:yam of Sa:nthi Parva explains the significance of this avatha:ra!

At the time of creation, Lord **S**ri:manna:ra:ya**n**a taught the Holy Ve:das to the four headed Bramha. While Bramha was being preached, the four Ve:das appeared in the form of four Ve:da Purushas - human beings. But, Bramha did not pay attention. Paying a deaf ear to one's teacher is a great sin! As a result, two demons Madhu and Kaitabha emerged from a drop of sweat that formed at the Lord's navel.

These demons tried to steal the Ve:das from Bramha. All the four Ve:da Purushas fought on behalf of Bramha, but they were of no match for the two demons. The demons carried the Ve:da Purushas away to the underworld, rasa:thala, leaving Bramha in his own world. What happens when light is lost? There will be dark-

ness. Similarly, having lost the light of knowledge and surrounded by darkness, Bramha prayed to the ord and performed a great yajna to get blessed by the Lord again with the nowledge of the Ve:das. Lord Sri:manna:ra:yana, who is compassionate, took pity on Bramha and went to the underworld rasa:thala in the form of Hayagri:va and neighed loudly.

The stentorian voice of Lord Hayagri:va frightened the demons and made them run helter - skelter in horror. Then, Lord Hayagri:va brought the Ve:da Purushas carefully from the underworld and appeared from the fire altar of the yajna that Bramha was performing. He blessed Bramha, who prayed earnestly for the divine knowledge again with the Ve:das. The neighing of Lord Hayagri:va resembles *udgi:ttha*, the music of Sa:ma Ve:da.

The demons who had run away previously, returned and searched for the Ve:da Purushas. As they failed to find them in the place where they hid them, they left for Vaikuntta, the abode of Lord Vishnu, wondering if they had been rescued by Him. Foolishly, they challenged Lord Vishnu for a fight and ended up losing their lives. But, Lord Vishnu is so compassionate that He cannot ignore even those that fight Him. He blessed them with salvation in spite of their sins.

As *Bramha* obtained the Vedic knowledge with all earnestness, he was able to retain it with him forever without any disturbance. That's why it is said that *'nothing should be taught without being requested'*. Lord Vishnu created Bramha on the day of *prathipath or pa:dyami*, the 1st day after new moon and preached him the divine knowledge of the Ve:das. As it all went futile, it has been suggested that a new lesson should not be taught or learnt on *prathipath or pa:dyami* day, i.e., the first day after new moon or full moon.

Since the Lord appeared on *Sra:vana Pu:rnima*, in the holy fire of *yajna*, He feels specially pleased with all our prayers on that day and blesses us with all love and compassion, as it is His birthday. He removes all our obstacles and blesses us with the most powerful and the greatest knowledge, which helps us achieve great results.

Our elders say that Lord Hayagri:va is the embodiment of all knowledge. *Haya* means knowledge and *gri:va* means the neck. Lord Hayagri:va is thus the personification of all divine knowledge.

The four Ve:da:s – *Ruk, Yajus, Sa:ma and Attharva* are the source for all knowledge in the world. They are in the form of *manthras*, the holy chants with verypow-

erful sounds. These manthras contain *bi:ja:ksharas*, vital letters. The entire energy of the manthra lies in these *bi:ja:ksharas*. The *bi:ja:ksharas* are subtle and indistinctive unlike the *manthras*. They do not appear meaningful, but possess excellent power. These *bi:ja:ksharas* are called *uththama:nga* of the *manthras*. '*uththama:nga*' means head. If we personify the manthras, Hayavadana is the head similar to the bi:ja:ksharas of the *manthras*.

It is difficult to guess the meaning of a horse's neighing! The meaning of the neighing of this great Hayavadana also appears to be inexplicable, but it has a divine meaning. It is very powerful like the *bi:ja:ksharas*. It eradicates all evils and hence the evil and diabolic forces ran hither and thither.

Though we are not able to chant all the *manthras* and the hidden *bi:ja:ksharas*, a sincere prayer to Lord Hayagri:va, the embodiment of all divine knowledge, will bring us all the power of learning. Sri Ve:da:ntha De:sika composed *Hayagri:va Stho:thra* in thirty three verses explaining the significance of Lord Hayagri:va.

The whole divine world of de:vathas has thirty three divisions. Similarly, the total number of letters in the holy *manthras ashta:kshari: & dwaya manthra* also are thirty three. The divine energy of each letter was embedded by *Sri Ve:da:ntha De:sika* in each verse. This was experienced by great scholars. Hence, this great *stho:thra* was revered by profound scholars in the past and also is being revered in the present for a great eloquence and powerful speech.

Let all the enthusiastic scholars and students chant these powerful verses for a great power ful eloquent speech with a strong grip on the words and their meanings through the benediction of Lord Hayagri:va!

Jai **S**rimanna:raya**n**a!

Telugu	Hindi	English	Telugu	Hindi	English
అ	अ	a	ట	ट	ta
ఆ	आ	a:	ఠ	ठ	tta
ఇ	इ	i	డ	ड	tta
ఈ	ई	i:	ఢ	ढ	da
ఉ	उ	u	ణ	ण	dda
ఊ	ऊ	u:			dha
ఋ	ऋ	ru	త	त	na
ౠ	ॠ	ru:	థ	थ	tha
ఌ	अलु	lu	ద	द	ththa
ౡ	अलू	lu:	ధ	ध	ttha
ఎ		e	న	न	da
ఏ	ए	e:			dda
ఐ	ऐ	ai			dha
ఒ		o			na
ఓ	ओ	o:	ప	प	pa
ఔ	औ	au/ow	ఫ	फ	pha
అం	अं	am	బ	ब	ba
అః	अः	aha	భ	भ	bha
క	क	ka	మ	म	ma
ఖ	ख	kha	య	य	ya
గ	ग	ga	ర	र	ra
ఘ	घ	gha	ల	ल	la
ఙ	ङ	nga	వ	व	va
చ	च	cha	శ	श	sa
ఛ	छ	chcha	ష	ष	sha
ఛ	छ	chha	స	स	sa
జ	ज	ja	హ	ह	ha
ఝ	झ	jha	ళ	ळ	la
ఞ	ञ	ini	ఱ		rra
			క్ష	क्ष	ksha
			జ్ఞ		Jna

• This letter comes only in the middle of the word
•• This letter comes in the beginning/middle of the word
☞ Pronounciation of both these letters is almost similar

Slo:ka:s to be chanted before starting Sri: Hayagri:va Stho:thram

sri:**s**aile:**s**a daya: pathram dhi:bhakthya:di gu**n**a:r**n**avam |
yathi:ndra prava**n**am vande: ramyaja:ma:tharam munim ||

lakshmi:na:ttha sama:rambha:m na:tthaya:muna madhyama:m |
asmada:cha:rya paryan:tha:m vande: guruparampara:m ||

yo:nithya machyutha pada:mbuja yugma rukma
vya:mo:hathas thadithara:**n**i thru**n**a:ya me:ne: |
asmadguro:r bhagavatho:sya dayaika sindho:ho
ra:ma:nujasya chara**n**au **s**ara**n**am prapadye: ||

ma:tha: pitha: yuvathaya sthanaya: vibhu:thihi
sarvam yade:va niyame:na madanvaya:na:m |
a:dyasya nah kulapathe: rvaku**l**a:bhira:mam
sri:math thadanghri yuga**l**am pra**n**ama:mi mu:rdhna: ||

bhu:tham sara**s**cha maha:da:hvaya bhattana:tta
sri:bhakthisa:ra kulase:khara yo:giva:ha:n |
bhaktha:nghrire:**n**u paraka:la yathi:ndra misra:n
sri:math para:mku**s**a munim pra**n**atho:smi nithyam ||

Sri: Hayagri:va Stho:thram

jna:na:nanda mayam de:vam nirmala sphatika:kruthim |
a:dha:ram sarva vidya:na:m hayagri:vam upa:smahe: || 1

swathassiddham **s**uddha sphatikama**n**i bhu:bhruth prathibhatam
sudha: sadhri:chi:bhihi dyuthibhiravada:tha thribhuvanam |
ananthaihi thrayyanthaihi anuvihitha he:sha: halahalam
hatha:**s**e:sha:vadyam hayavadanam i:di:mahi mahaha || 2

sama:ha:ras sa:mna:m prathipadam rucha:m dha:ma yajusha:m
layah prathyu:ha:na:m lahari vithathir bo:dha jaladhe:he |
kattha:darpa kshubhyath katthaka kula ko:la:hala bhavam
harathvanthar dhwa:ntham hayavadana he:sha: hala halaha || 3

pra:chi:sandhya: ka:chi danthar nisa:ya:ha
prajna: drushte:r anjana sri:r apu:rva: |
vakthri: ve:da:n bha:thu me: va:jivakthra:
va:gi:sa:khya: va:sude:vasya mu:rthihi || 4

visuddha vijna:na ghana swaru:pam
vijna:na visra:nana baddha di:ksham |
daya:nidhim de:ha bhrutha:m saranyam
de:vam hayagri:vam aham prapadye: || 5

apaurushe:yai:r api va:kprapanchaihi
adya:pi the: bhu:thim adrushtapa:ra:m |
sthuvannaham mugdha ithi thwayaiva
ka:runyatho: na:ttha! kata:kshani:yaha || 6

da:kshinya ramya: girisasya mu:rthihi
de:vi: saro:ja:sana dharma pathni: |
vya:sa:dayo:pi vyapade:sya va:chaha
sphuranthi sarve: thava sakthi le:saihi || 7

mando: bhavishyan niyatham virincho:
va:cha:m nidhe:! vanchitha bha:gadhe:yaha |
dai:thya:pani:tha:n dayayai:va bhu:yo:pi
adhya:payishyo: nigama:n nache:ththvam || 8

vitharka do:la:m vyavadhu:ya saththve:
bruhaspathim varthayase: yathas thvam |
the:nai:va de:va! thridase:swara:na:m
asprushta do:la:yitham a:dhira:jyam || 9

agnau samiddha:rchishi saptha thantho:ho
a:thastthiva:n manthramayam sari:ram |
akhandasa:rair havisha:m prada:naihi
a:pya:yanam vyo:masada:m vidhathse: || 10

yanmu:lam i:druk prathibha:thi thaththwam
ya:mu:lam a:mna:ya maha:druma:na:m |

thaththwe:na ja:nanthi visuddha saththwa:ha
tha:m akshara:m akshara ma:thruka:nthe: || 11

avya:krutha:th vya:kruthava:nasi thwam
na:ma:ni ru:pa:ni cha ya:ni pu:rvam |
samsanthi the:sha:m charama:m prathishtta:m
va:gi:swara! thwa:m thwadupajna va:chaha || 12

mugdhe:ndu nishyanda vilo:bhani:ya:m
mu:rthim thava:nanda sudha: prasu:thim |
vipaschithas che:thasi bha:vayanthe:
ve:la:m uda:ra:m iva dugdha sindho:ho || 13

mano:gatham pasyathi yassada: thwa:m
mani:shi:na:m ma:nasa ra:jahamsam |
swayam puro:bha:va viva:dabha:jaha
kim kurvathe: thasya giro: yattha:rham || 14

api kshana:rttham kalayanthi ye: thwa:m
a:pla:vayantham visadair mayu:khaihi |
va:cha:m prava:hair aniva:rithais the:
manda:kini:m mandayithum kshamanthe: || 15

swa:min! bhavad dhya:na sudha:bhishe:ka:th
vahanthi dhanya:h pulaka:nu bandham |
alakshithe: kwa:pi nirudhamu:lam
ange:shviv a:nandadhum ankurantham || 16

swa:min prathi:cha: hrudaye:na dhanya:ha
thwad dhya:na chandro:daya vardhama:nam |
ama:ntham a:nanda payo:dhi manthaha
payo:bhi rakshna:m pariva:hayanthi || 17

swaira:nu bha:va:s thwadadhi:na bha:va:ha
samruddhavi:rya:s thwadanu grahe:na |
vipaschitho: na:ttha! tharanthi ma:ya:m
vaiha:riki:m mo:hana pinchhika:m the: || 18

pra:ng nirmitha:na:m thapasa:m vipa:ka:h
prathyagra nissre:yasa sampado: me: |
same:dhishi:rams thava pa:dapadme:
sankalpa chintha:manayah prana:ma:ha || 19

viluptha mu:rdhanya lipi krama:**n**a:m
sure:ndra chu:da:pada la:litha:na:m |
thvadanghri ra:ji:va rajah ka**n**a:na:m
bhu:ya:n prasa:do: mayi na:ttha! bhu:ya:th || 20

parisphuran nu:pura chithrabha:nu
praka:**s**a nirdhu:tha thamo:nushanga:m |
pada dwayi:m the: parichin mahe:nthaha
prabo:dha ra:ji:va vibha:tha sandhya:m || 21

thwath kinkara:lankara**n**o:chitha:na:m
thwayaiva kalpa:nthara pa:litha:na:m |
manju pra**n**a:dam ma**n**inu:puram the:
manju:shika:m ve:dagira:m prathi:maha || 22

sanchinthaya:mi prathibha: da**s**a:sttha:n
sandhukshayantham samaya pradi:pa:n |
vijna:na kalpadruma pallava:bham
vya:khya:namudra: madhuram karam the: || 23

chiththe: karo:mi sphuritha:ksha ma:lam
savye:tharam na:ttha! karam thwadi:yam |
jna:na:mrutho:danchana la:lasa:na:m
li:la:ghati: yanthra miva:**s**ritha:na:m || 24

prabo:dhasindho:r arunai:h praka:**s**aihi
prava:**l**a sangha:tha mivo:dvahantham |
vibha:vaye: de:va! sapusthakam the:
va:mam karam dakshi**n**am a:**s**ritha:na:m || 25

thama:msi bhithva: vi**s**adair mayu:khaihi
sampri:**n**ayantham vidusha**s** chako:ra:n |
ni**s**a:maye: thwa:m nava pu**n**dari:ke:
saradghane: chandram iva sphurantham || 26

di**s**anthu me: de:va! sada: thwadi:ya:ha
daya:tharanga:nu chara:h kata:ksha:ha |
sro:thre:shu pumsa:m amrutham ksharanthi:m
saraswathi:m sam**s**ritha ka:madhe:num || 27

vi:se:shavith pa:rishade:shu na:ttha
vidagdha go:shtti: samara:ngane:shu |
jigi:shatho: me: kavitha:rki ke:ndra:n
jihva:gra simha:sanam abhyupe:ya:ha || 28

thwa:m chinthayan thvanmayatha:m prapannaha
thwa:mudgrunan sabdamaye:na dha:mna: |
swa:min sama:je:shu same:dhishi:ya
swachhanda va:da:hava baddhasu:raha || 29

na:na: vidha:na:m agathih kala:na:m
nacha:pi thi:rtthe:shu krutha:vatha:raha |
dhruvam thawa:na:ttha parigraha:ya:ha
navam navam pa:thram aham daya:ya:ha || 30

akampani:ya: nyapani:thi bhe:daihi
alankrushi:ran hrudayam madi:yam |
sanka: kalanka:paga mo:jjwala:ni
thaththwa:ni samyanchi thawa prasa:da:th || 31

vya:khya: mudra:m kara sarasijaih pusthakam sankha chakre:
bibhrad bhinna sphatika ruchire: pundari:ke: nishannaha |
amla:na sri:r amrutha visadair amsubhih pla:vayanma:m
a:virbhu:ya:d anagha mahima: ma:nase: va:gadhi:saha || 32

va:garttha siddhi he:tho:h pattatha
hayagri:va samsthuthim bhakthya: |
kavitha:rkika ke:sarina:
ve:nkatana:tthe:na virachitha:m e:tha:m || 33

kavitha:rkika simha:ya kalya:na gunasa:line: |
sri:mathe: ve:nkate:sa:ya ve:da:ntha gurave: namaha ||

Sri: Hayagri:va Mangala:sasanam

sarva vidya: swaru:pa:ya lakshmi: samslishta vakshase: |
madupa:sana lakshya:ya hayagri:va:ya mangalam ||

sri: hayagri:va parabramhane: namaha
Jai Sri:manna:ra:yana!!

SRI: HAYAGRI:VA STHO:THRAM

jna:na:nanda mayam de:vam nirmala sphatika:kruthim |
a:dha:ram sarva vidya:na:m hayagri:vam upa:smahe: || 1

upa:smahe:	= I meditate upon
Hayagri:vam	= the Horse - necked
de:vam	= bright God
a:dha:ram	= the source
sarva + vidya:na:m	= of all masteries
a:kruthim	= the form of whom
nirmala	= shines spotless
sphatika	= like a white crystal
jna:na + a:nanda + mayam	
mayam	= filled with
jna:na	= eternal knowledge and
a:nandam	= eternal bliss

Lord Hayagri:va has a resplendent treasure of infinite knowledge which illuminates the whole world. This knowledge fulfills the desires of all the people and hence it is useful for all. The thing which is practically useful, gives us the real joy. Lord Hayagri:va is the personification of *knowledge* and *joy*. That is why he shineswith a greater brilliance than that of the sun and the moon. Hence, we worship Lord Hayagri:va, who is the embodiment of all knowledge and who shines like an immaculate pure crystal gem.

Chant this slo:ka to get good education.

swathassiddham suddha sphatikamani bhu:bhruth prathibhatam
sudha: sadhri:chi:bhihi dyuthibhiravada:tha thribhuvanam |
ananthaihi thrayyanthaihi anuvihita he:sha: halahalam
hatha:se:sha:vadyam hayavadanam i:di:mahi mahaha || 2

i:di:mahi = we praise
mahaha = the divine glow
haya+vadanam = called Hayavadana, the horse-necked God
1. siddham = who appeared
   swathaha = on his own
2. prathi+bhatam = competing
   bhu:bruth = with a mountain
   sphatika+mani = made of crystal gem
   suddha = which is pure
3. avada:tha + thri + bhuvanam
   avada:tha = shining
   thri = all the three
   bhuvanam = worlds
   dhyuthibhihi = with the glowing rays emitting from his form

sudha: + sadhri:chi:bhihi
sadri:chi:bhihi = which are equal to
sudha: = the glow that radiates from the white plastering
4. anuvihitha + he:sha: + halahalam
   halahalam = the loud noise
   he:sha: = of whose neigh
   anuvihitha = is being followed
   ananthaihi = by countless
   thrayyanthaihi = Upanishads
5. hatha + ase:sha + avadyam
   hatha = which destroys
   avadyam = defects
   ase:sha = of all devotees

Lord Hayagri:va is a magnificent beam of divine radiance. He appeared at his own will. Only with a benevolent heart and without any evocation he took a visible form. His radiance competes with the shining mountain of spotless crystal gems. The pure brilliance of his body, like the radiating splendor of a painted white wall in bright light, spreads all over the world and makes the three worlds sparkle with knowledge. He is the epitome of all wisdom. He removes the darkness of ignorance from the three worlds and bestows the light of knowledge on them. Even the Upanishads echo his loud neighing. We worship this Hayagri:va, this divine beam of light, which removes several vicious symptoms like foolishness etc.,

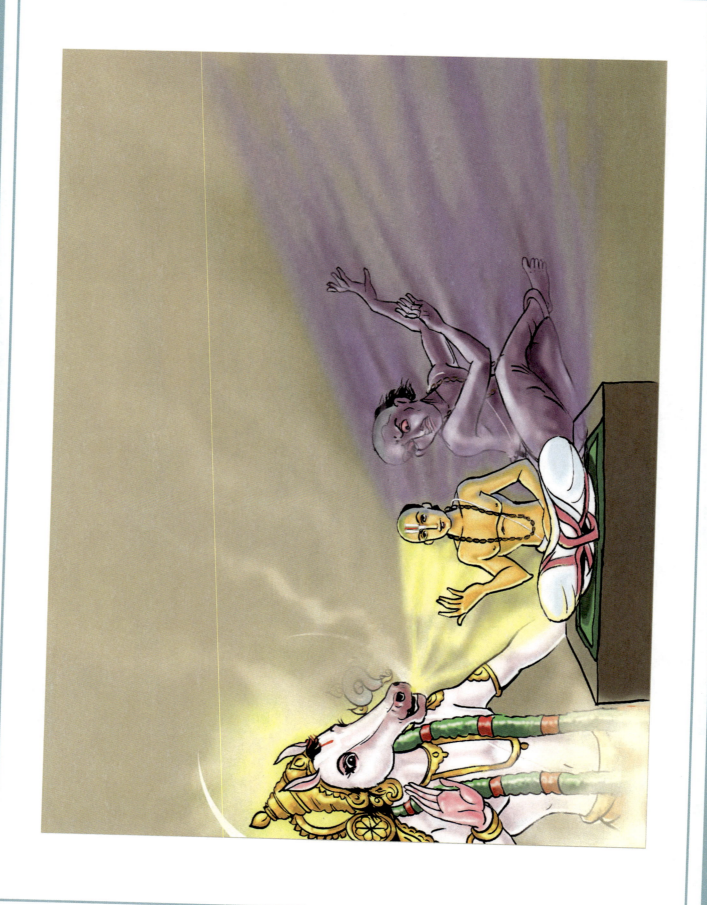

sama:ha:ras sa:mna:m prathipadam rucha:m dha:ma yajusha:m
layah prathyu:ha:na:m lahari vithathir bo:dha jaladhe:he |
kattha:darpa kshubhyath katthaka kula ko:la:hala bhavam
harathvanthar dhwa:ntham hayavadana he:sha: hala halaha || 3

he reverberating noise
he:sha = of the neigh
Haya+vadana = from the Lord Haya Gri:va
a. sama:ha:raha = the collection
sa:mna:m = of the tunes of Sa:ma ve:da
b. prathipadam = a synonym
rucha:m = of splendorous hymns of Rug Ve:da
c. dha:ma = the abode
yajusha:m = of sacrificial formulae of Yajur Ve:da
d. layaha = the destroyer
prathyu:ha:na:m = of obstacles
e. vithathihi = the cascade

lahari = of waves
jaladhe:he = from the ocean
bo:dha = of knowledge
harathu = may dispel
anthar + dhwa:ntham= inner darkness, the ignorance
bhavam = caused
ko:la:hala = by the commotion
katthaka + kula = from the crowd of opponents
kshyubhyath = who are frantic
darpa = out of arrogance
kattha = due to pretentious & hollow arguments

The Personification of all the Ve:das! The Protector from the darkness of ignorance! Lord Hayagri:va! Your splendid voice made the demons run helter-skelter. May the neighing sound of your voice remove our diabolic attitudes and give us the divine knowledge!

Your voice embodies the sonorous music of the Vedas. It manifests the collection of the tunes of the *Sa:mave:da*. It synonymously stands for the splendorous hymns of the *Rugve:da*. It will give us great skills to please all people, as the *'ruks'* of the Rugve:da appease the divinity with its praising verses. As your voice is the abode of the sacred and sacrificial chants of the *Yajurve:da*, and as it proves all the yagnas as your worship, your reverberating neighing will transform all our acts as the worship of God. Your divine voice resembles the waves in the ocean of knowledge. It removes all obstacles faced by us, your devotees. It sweeps all our doubts away and gives us the right knowledge. Those who are knowledgeable and wise must help and enlighten those who are dull and low. But some arrogant people behave in a different and pretentious way. They always oppose, argue and create a lot of disturbance frantically. Ordinary people follow, fall a prey to them and praise such braggarts and become a part of such imprudent crowds. May your resonant voice remove such weakness and ignorance of all!

**pra:chi:sandhya: ka:chi danthar nisa:ya:ha
prajna: drushte:r anjana sri:r apu:rva: |
vakthri: ve:da:n bha:thu me: va:jivakthra:
va:gi:sa:khya: va:sude:vasya mu:rthihi ||** 4

	mu:rthihi	= Let the Divine Form
	va:sude:vasya	= of Sri:manna:ra:yana
a.	va:k + i:sa + a:khya:	= the renowned lord of speech
b.	va:ji + vakthra:	= whose voice is like a horse
c.	vakthri:	= who reveals
	ve:da:n	= Ve:das
d.	apu:rva:	= The Unique
	anjana + sri:hi	= bright kohl (eyeliner)
	prajna + druste:he:	= to the inner knowledge
e.	ka:chit	= The magnificent
	pra:chi:	= eastern
	sandhya:	= sunrise
	anthar + nisa:ya:ha	= to the inner ignorance
	bha:thu	= appear
	me:	= to me

The divine form of Lord Hayagri:va, whose voice is like that of a horse, is the magnificent eastern aurora culminating the dark night of mind's ignorance. It is the exceptional kohl, the eye-lining balm for the blooming eye of wisdom. May this celestial form of Sri:manna:ra:yana, which reveals the Ve:das as its breath and which owns all speech skills and knowledge, appear as my guiding light!

Chant this slo:ka to get rid of ignorance.

visuddha vijna:na ghana swaru:pam
vijna:na visra:nana baddha di:ksham |
daya:nidhim de:ha bhrutha:m saranyam
de:vam hayagri:vam aham prapadye: || 5

	aham	= I
	prapadye:	= surrender
	Hayagri:vam	= to Haya gri:va
	de:vam	= the divine lord
a.	ghana	= the personification
	visuddha	= of pure
	vijna:na	= knowledge
	swaru:pam	= as His form
b.	baddha + di:ksham	= the One sworn
	visra:nana	= to bestow
	vijna:na	= the Real Knowledge
c.	daya: + nidhim	= the treasure chest of compassion
d.	saranyam	= The Protector
	de:ha + bhrutha:m	= to all the creatures

I bow and surrender myself to Lord Hayagri:va, who is the embodiment of pure knowledge, who has unswerving will in bestowing the real wisdom, who is the treasure house of compassion and who is the Savior of all the creatures.

Mankind often possesses any or all the four kinds of deficiencies, *bhrama, prama:da, vipralipsa and asakthi*. *Bhrama* is misconception; *prama:da* is lack of concentration; *vipralipsa* is the desire to deceive others and *asakthi* is the inability to perceive and express. Lord Hayagri:va removes all such deficiencies and blesses us with accurate knowledge.

apaurushe:yai:r api va:kprapanchaihi
adya:pi the: bhu:thim adrushtapa:ra:m |
sthuvannaham mugdha ithi thwayaiva
ka:ru**n**yatho: na:ttha! kata:ksha**n**i:yaha || 6

Na:ttha !	= Oh Lord!
aham	= I
sthuvan	= dare to eulogize
bhu:thim	= the wealth
the:	= of yours
adrushta + pa:ra:m	= which is incomprehensible
api	= even
adya	= till date
api	= even
apaurushe:yaihi:	= by the eternal
va:k + prapanchaihi	= and vastly spread ve:dic hymns
kata:kshani:yaha	= hence, I must be considered
ithi	= as
mugdhaha	= an innocent child
thwaya:	= by you
ka:runyathaha + e:va	= only out of compassion

Lord Hayagri:va! The Holy Ve:das are not written by anybody. Hence, they have neither partiality nor hatred towards anyone. Even those Ve:das have failed to describe your greatness. I am venturing to eulogize your inexplicable magnificence without any fear. It is mere childishness to make such an attempt. Please, pardon my mistake. Be compassionate and bear with my ignorance.

**da:kshinya ramya: girisasya mu:rthihi
de:vi: saro:ja:sana dharma pathni: |
vya:sa:dayo:pi vyapade:sya va:chaha
sphuranthi sarve: thava sakthi le:saihi || 7**

ramya:	= An attractive
mu:rthihi	= form
girisasya	= of Sankara
da:kshinya	= called Dakshina: Mu:rthy, capable of imparting knowledge
dharma + pathni:	= The divine consort of
saro:ja + a:sana	= Bramha, who is seated on a lotus
de:vi:	= Va:gde:vi, also called Saraswathi, the Goddess of words
api	= even
sarve:	= all
vyapade:sya + va:chaha	= the renowned scholars
vya:sa + a:dayaha	= like Ve:da Vya:sa and others
sphuranthi	= are shining
sakthi + le:saihi	= only with the fraction of powerful grace
thava	= of yours

There are some de:vathas and sages who bestowed and continue to bestow knowledge on the human beings. The attractive form of Lord Siva, who is called *Dakshina: Mu:rthy*, capable of imparting knowledge, dwells in a part of Your Divine Form.

Bramha was born in the Lotus from Your Naval. His divine consort Va:gde:vi, also called Saraswathi, is another de:vatha to grant knowledge. The Great Sage Ve:da Vya:sa divided the Holy Ve:das, wrote 18 great Pura:nas, and authored the Bramha Su:thras.

All these have become great due to an iota of your infinite grace alone. Lord Hayagri:va, I humbly pray to You to mold me similarly.

Chant this slo:ka to become a good fluent speaker.

mando: bhavishyan niyatham virincho:
va:cha:m nidhe:! vanchitha bha:gadhe:yaha |
dai:thya:pani:tha:n dayayai:va bhu:yo:pi
adhya:payishyo: nigama:n nache:ththvam || 8

va:cha:m + nidhe:	= Oh Haya gri:va! The treasure house of knowledge
virinchaha	= The four headed Bramha
abhavishyath	= would have been
mandaha	= ignorant
niyatham	= and for sure
vanchitha	= deprived
bhagadhe:yaha	= of wealth
bhu:yaha + api	= once again
che:th	= if
thwam	= you
dayaya: + e:va	= only out of compassion
na adhya:payishyaha	= had not taught
nigama:n	= Ve:das
apani:tha:n	= that were snatched
daithya	= by the demons

Lord Hayagri:va, the treasure house of all knowledge! You imparted the Holy Ve:das to the four headed Bramha at the time of creation. He did not listen to that attentively. As a result, the Ve:das were taken away by the demons called Madhu and Kaitabha. Then Lord Bramha realized the importance of the Ve:das and started repenting. To console him and to restore the lost treasure of knowledge, You appeared in the form of Haya - Gri:va. You destroyed those demons. You taught all those Ve:das to Bramha with all patience! Bramha would not have been a bright and intelligent creator, had you not blessed him again with that real knowledge! He would have been an ignoramus, deprived of Ve:dic wealth. O Lord Hayagri:va! Make us knowledgeable and wise. Bless us with good speaking skills.

Chant this slo:ka to attain a higher postion at work and for a prosperous life.

vitharka do:la:m vyavadhu:ya saththve:
bruhaspathim varthayase: yathas thvam |
the:nai:va de:va! thridase:swara:na:m
asprushta do:la:yitham a:dhira:jyam || 9

De:va !	= oh Luminous Lord Hayagri:va!
yathaha	= as
thwam	= you
vyavadhu:ya	= are eradicating
vitharka + do:la:m	= the wavering & unclear thoughts
bruhaspathim	= of Bruhaspathi
the:na	= then
vartha yase:	= keeping him
saththve: + eva	= only in sathva guna, the pure state of mind
a:dhira:jyam	= the empire
thri + dasa + i:swara:na:m	= of de:vathas
asprushta + do:la:yitham	= remain untouched from vacillation

   O Luminous Lord Hayagri:va! Sage Bruhaspathi was able to gain divine knowledge only due to Your grace. As you eradicated his wavering and unstable thoughts, he was able to win over bad qualities such as anger. You blessed him with *sathva guna*, the tranquil state of mind. It is due to this knowledge, Bruhaspathi is able to guide de:vathas to maintain their abode peacefully, without any disturbance. Even that Bruhaspathi acquired his abilities from Your abundant grace! We request You to bless us with a similar state of mind and with the fruit of steady success!

agnau samiddha:rchishi saptha thantho:ho
a:thastthiva:n manthramayam sari:ram |
akhandasa:rair havisha:m prada:naihi
a:pya:yanam vyo:masada:m vidhathse: || 10

thwam	= you
a:thastthiva:n	= have accepted
sari:ram	= a divine body
manthra + mayam	= made of manthras
samiddha:rchishi	= with blazing flames
agnou	= in the fire
saptha + thantho:ho	= from Ya:ga, the sacred Rituals.
vidhathse:	= You permit
a:pya:yanam	= nourishment
vyo:masada:m	= to de:vathas, the celestials in heavens
prada:naihi	= by delivering
havisha:m	= the oblations
akhanda + sa:raihi	= which are full of essence, as You are the inner power.

Lord Hayagri:va, you offer satiety to hundreds of thousands of celestial beings including Bramha and Bruhaspathi. The sacrificial food offered to the celestial beings through *yajnas*, becomes acceptable only when it is offered along with proper *manthras*; otherwise, it becomes futile. It is due to the chanting of those manthras, the sacrificial offerings to de:vathas acquire a pleasing taste and energy. Since You dwell in the divine manthras and support them, they acquire such energy!

**yanmu:lam i:druk prathibha:thi thaththwam
ya:mu:lam a:mna:ya maha:druma:na:m |
thaththwe:na ja:nanthi visuddha saththwa:ha
tha:m akshara:m akshara ma:thruka:nthe: || 11**

thathvam	= the entire real world
prathibha:thi	= perceived
i:druk	= as combination of nature and the souls
yath + mu:lam	= has its roots in the letter 'A';
ya:	= the same letter 'A'
mu:lam	= is the origin
a:mna:ya + maha: + druma:na:m	= of the eternal trees called A:mna:ya, the holy Ve:das;
visuddha + sathva:ha	= the enlightened and the wise
ja:nanthi	= are realizing
thathve:na	= in all true sense
tha:m	= that causal
akshara:m	= eternal letter 'A'
akshara + ma:thruka:m	= divine mother of all letters and The Ve:das
the:	= denotes You as The Supreme

The enlightened and the wise have realized that all the animate and inanimate objects in this creation have emerged from the first syllable of the divine sound $O:m$, i.e, 'a', as $O:m$ is a combination of $a+u+m$. The Universe consists of Prama:nas and Prame:yas.

Prame:yas means 'all the objects that can be perceived'. They are celestial beings, humans, birds, animals, trees, stones etc. In other words, they are all the animate and inanimate objects of this Universe. Prama:nam is the whole Ve:dic Literature that elucidates the above objects and more.

All the objects emerge from the Lord and eventually culminate in Him. Similarly, the entire literature originates from the divine syllable 'a', and finally, dissolves in it only. Now, it is clear that the Lord and 'A' remain eternal, as the Indicated and the Indicator. So, they both are inseparable and called 'akshara ma:thruka'. Akshara means 'indestructible'. Ma:thruka means 'source'. Thus, O Hayagri:va! The enlightened sages and wise have established that You are the real meaning of that letter 'a'.

avya:krutha:th vya:kruthava:nasi thwam
na:ma:ni ru:pa:ni cha ya:ni pu:rvam |
samsanthi the:sha:m charama:m prathishtta:m
va:gi:swara! thwa:m thwadupajna va:chaha || 12

Vagi:swara	= Oh Lord Hayagri:va!
upajna + va:chaha	= great seers, blessed with the Supreme initial knowledge
thwath	= from you
samsanthi	= are realizing
thwa:m	= You
charama:m	= as the ultimate
prathishtta:m	= abode
the:sha:m	= to all those objects
ya:ni	= which
thwam	= you
vya:kruthava:n + asi	= have outstretched
na:ma:ni	= as objects with names
ru:pa:ni + cha	= also with structures and characteristics
avya:krutha:th	= from a state where these details were too small to see
pu:rvam	= earlier

Lord Hayagri:va, the whole world was in a state of deluge and was in an indivisible state/shape without a form or name in the beginning. You divided it into many forms and gave them names. You protected their minute forms and nourished / nurtured them when You felt that they should grow. The different changes of all the animate and inanimate things and objects from 'avya:krutha' (invisible) state to 'vya:krutha' (visible) state and again to 'avya:krutha' state are due to Your Will. These forms and names remain unchanged even at the end as they have all originated/emanated from You! The great seers who acquired their supreme wisdom from the Holy Ve:das through Your abundant grace realised this!

**mugdhe:ndu nishyanda vilo:bhani:ya:m
mu:rthim thava:nanda sudha: prasu:thim |
vipaschithas che:thasi bha:vayanthe:
ve:la:m uda:ra:m iva dugdha sindho:ho || 13**

vipaschithaha	= the erudite scholars
bha:vayanthe:	= meditate upon
thava	= your
mu:rthihi	= Divine Form
che:thasi	= in their heart

a. mugdha + indu + nishyanda + vilo:bhani:ya:m
    vilo:bhani:ya:m = which is glamorous
    nishyanda = like the gush of moon light
    mugdha + indu = from the full moon

b. a:nanda + sudha: + prasu:thim
    prasu:thim = the fountain head
    sudha: = of the nectar
    a:nanda = that provides divine bliss

iva	= which is like
uda:ra:m	= bewitching
ve:la:m	= shore
dugdha + sindho:ho	= of Milky Ocean

    Lord Hayagri:va! Your beautiful/magnificent form is a feast to the eyes! It is like the overflowing soft stream of bright light from the moon. It is like the fountain head of joyous nectar of divine bliss. It is like the enchanting shore of the Milky Ocean. Thus, all erudite scholars meditate upon Your celestial form in their hearts!

Chant this slo:ka to speak spontaneously.

mano:gatham pa**s**yathi yassada: thwa:m
mani:shi:**n**a:m ma:nasa ra:jahamsam |
swayam puro:bha:va viva:dabha:jaha
kim kurvathe: thasya giro: yattha:rham || 14

giraha	= languages
puraha + bha:va + viva:da +bha:jaha	= passionately (as if competing to stand in front of him)
Kim + kurvathe:	= extend services
swayam	= on their own
yattha:rham	= at the beck and call
thasya	= to him
yaha	= the one who
sada:	= always
pasyathi	= visualizes
thwa:m	= you
manaha +gatham	= the indweller of the heart,
ma:nasa +ra:ja + hamsam	= as the king of swans in the hearts
mani:shina:m	= of great devotees

Lord Hayagri:va! The heart of Your true devotee, who always meditates on You with all faith and sincerity, becomes a placid lake in which You move like a graceful Royal Swan! He who sees You in his heart and worships You with all faith forever, will have all the languages at his beck and call. They compete to stand before him for being possessed. Such people never fumble for words. Dear Lord! I pray to You to be a Royal Swan in our hearts and make us eloquent.

Chant this slo:ka for eloquent powerful speech.

apiksha**n**a:rttham kalayanthi ye: thwa:m
a:pla:vayantham vi**s**adair mayu:khaihi |
va:cha:m prava:hair aniva:rithais the:
manda:kini:m mandayithum kshamanthe: || 15

the:	= those devotees
kshamanthe:	= are capable
mandayithum	= of slowing down
manda:kini:m	= the flow of River Ganga
prava:haihi	= with the perfect flow
va:cha:m	= of communication
aniva:rithaihi	= having no blockades,
ye:	= whoever
kalayanthi	= affectionately serve
thwa:m	= you
a:pla:vayantham	= the Lord, who drenches the devotees
visadaihi	= with chaste
mayu:khaihi	= rays of grace
kshana +arttham + api	= even for a split second

Lord Hayagri:va! You are a benevolent Lord. You will drench all Your devotees with pious rays of grace even if they pray to You for a fraction of a second. You bless them with a great flow of eloquence. Even the swift flow of Sacred River Ganga, cannot match their fluency. This uninterrupted flow of language is possible only with Your unparalleled compassion.

**swa:min! bhavad dhya:na sudha:bhishe:ka:th
vahanthi dhanya:h pulaka:nu bandham |
alakshithe: kwa:pi niru:dhamu:lam
ange:shviv a:nandadhum ankurantham ||**   16

swa:min	= Oh Hayagri:va, the Lord of whole Universe
dhanya:ha	= the blessed
vahanthi	= are experiencing
pulaka + anubandham	= uninterrupted goose bumps
abhishe:ka:th	= by taking shower
sudha	= in the nectar
bhavath	= of your
dhya:na	= meditation
iva	= as though
a:namdadhum	= the bliss
ankurantham	= is sprouting
ange:shu	= from all parts of the body
niru:dha + mu:lam	= from a strong rooted inner source
kwa + api	= somewhere
alakshithe:	= though undetectable

Oh Hayagri:va! The Lord of knowledge and learning! Your blessed devotees are experiencing a rare, ecstatic and uninterrupted joy during their meditation. You are showering ambrosial grace on them as an unseen source. This joy can be seen sprouting from each and every cell of their bodies.

**swa:min prathi:cha: hrudaye:na dhanya:ha
thwad dhya:na chandro:daya vardhama:nam |
ama:ntham a:nanda payo:dhi manthaha
payo:bhi rakshna:m pariva:hayanthi ||**   17

Swa:min	= Oh Lord Hayagri:va!
dhanya:ha	= those well off in Your grace
hrudaye:na	= attaining pure heart
prathi:cha	= as a result of their inward journey
pariva:hayanthi	= bursting out
a:nanda + payo:dhim	= the ocean of joy
ama:ntham	= irrepressible
anthaha	= within them
payo:bhihi	= through the waters
akshna:m	= in their eyes
vardhama:nam	= which arise
dhya:na	= by deep meditation
thwath	= upon You
udaya	= like the appearance
chandra	= of moon (to the ocean)

Lord Hayagri:va, the pure hearts of the devotees who are blessed by Your grace always experience the internal bliss of joy. That ocean of joy always swells due to the ever rising moon of meditation. The ocean of joy overflows through their eyes in the form of tears as it cannot be repressed in the heart. Lord Hayagri:va! Your devotees always experience such great thrill and are blessed forever by You! Please bless us all with that same grace!

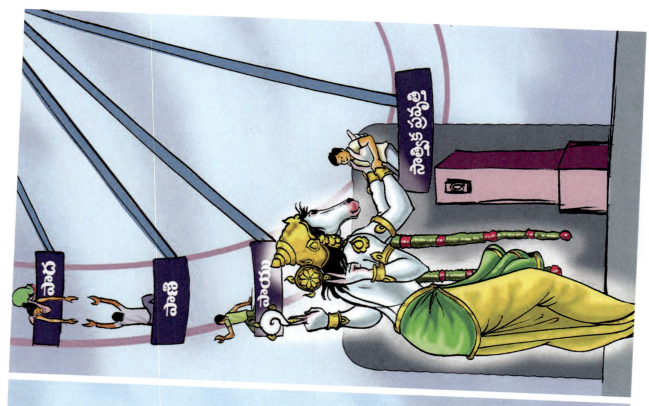

swaira:nu bha:va:s thwadadhi:na bha:va:ha
samruddhavi:rya:s thwadanu grahe:na |
vipaschitho: na:ttha! tharanthi ma:ya:m
vaiha:riki:m mo:hana pinchhika:m the: || 18

na:ttha!	= Oh Lord Hayavadana!
vipaschithaha	= the all knowing wise
swai:ra + anubha:va:ha	= who are able to soar in their intellectual heights
thwath + adhi:na + bha:va:ha	= dedicating their entire focus towards You
samruddha + vi:rya:ha	= and having command over their wisdom
thwath + anugrahe:na	= by Your mere grace
tharanthi	= are surpassing
ma:ya:m	= the mysterious inert Nature
the:	= of yours
mo:hana+pinchhika:m	= which is like a hypnotic wand
vaiha:riki:m	= which is also like your favorite place

O Benevolent Lord! Even those wise men who can soar high in the skies of great intellectual worlds submit their powers and thoughts at Your feet and meditate on Your form in their hearts. They are able to surpass this mysterious and inert nature, only due to Your grace. This mysterious and inert world which hypnotizes all the creatures is under Your control and acts at Your will. Only Your devotees can prevent that and can overcome its mesmerizing mysterious powers. O Lord Hayagri:va! Please bless us all with such abilities!

pra:ng nirmitha:na:m thapasa:m vipa:ka:h
prathyagra ni**ss**re:yasa sampado: me: |
same:dhishi:rams thava pa:dapadme:
sankalpa chintha:ma**n**ayah pra**n**a:ma:ha ||

19

    prana:ma:ha   = Let the prostrations
    me: = of mine
    a. sankalpa + chintha:manayaha
              = which fulfils the desires like Chintha:mani, the divine gems
    b. prathyagra + nissre:yasa + sampadaha
        sampadaha   = which are like riches
        nissre:yasa   = leading towards bliss
        prathyagra   = that is eternal
    c. vipa:ka:ha   = which are results of penances
    nirmitha:na:m   = done
    pra:k   = in the past life
    same:dhishi:ran   = progress
    pa:da + padme: = at the lotus feet
    thava   = of yours

Lord Hayagri:va, I am able to pray to You only due to the privileged penances of my past lives. Let this service be my goal forever, as eternal fruit. Meanwhile, let these prayers fulfill all the desires, like the divine gems called *Chintha:mani*, to serve You, to Your World and to Your devotees. May these prayers grow in abundance at Your lotus feet forever, and bless me with the eternal bliss of salvation!

viluptha mu:rdhanya lipi krama:nam
sure:ndra chu:da:pada la:litha:na:m |
thvadanghri ra:ji:va rajah kana:na:m
bhu:ya:n prasa:do: mayi na:ttha! bhu:ya:th || 20

bhu:ya:th	= Let there be
bhu:ya:n	= abundant
prasa:daha	= grace
rajaha + kana:na:m	= of dust particles
thwath + anghri + ra:ji:va	= of your lotus feet
mayi:	= on me
a. la:litha:na:m	= which are adorned
chu:da:pada	= on the heads
sure:ndra	= of de:vatha+s like Indra
b. viluptha	= which erase
lipi + krama:na:m	= the structured records, the destined fate
mu:rdhanya	= from our heads

O Lord Hayagri:va! May the holy dust of Your lotus-like tender feet grace me forever! All the de:vathas adorn their heads with it by bowing at Your feet. It removes the evil fate written on our foreheads. May such holy dust keep us inseparable from You even in our thoughts and give us success in all our endeavors!

parisphuran nu:pura chithrabha:nu
praka:**s**a nirdhu:tha thamo:nushanga:m |
pada dwayi:m the: parichin mahe:nthaha
prabo:dha ra:ji:va vibha:tha sandhya:m || 21

parichinmahe:	= we meditate upon
the:	= your
pada + dwayi:m	= pair of foot
anthaha	= in our hearts

a. prabo:dha + ra:ji:va + vibha:tha + sandhya:m
    sandhya:m = as the orange sky
    vibha:tha = of the early hours
    ra:ji:va = is to the lotus
    prabo:dha = that is about to blossom
(the orange color of the feet should blossom my heart with knowledge)

b. nirdhu:tha = which dispels
    thamaha + anushanga:m = inner ignorance
    praka:sa = with the radiance
    nu:pura = of the anklets
    parisphurath = which dazzles
    chithrabha:nu = like the sun

Lord Hayagri:va, we constantly meditate upon Your divine feet in our minds. Your feet resemble the lotus flowers of wisdom and they have the glowing anklets above them. These anklets shine like the rising sun with a golden aurora gleam! They dispel our darkness of ignorance. The splendorous radiance of Your feet alone can eradicate the ignorance of our minds and make our hearts bloom like the lotus flowers. Lord Hayagri:va, bless us to meditate upon your radiant feet forever!

thwath kinkara:lankarano:chitha:na:m
thwayaiva kalpa:nthara pa:litha:na:m |
manju prana:dam maninu:puram the:
manju:shika:m ve:dagira:m prathi:maha ||

22

prathi:maha	= we realize
mani + nu:puram	= the anklet bell
the:	= of yours
manju:shika:m	= as a decorated chest
ve:dagira:m	= to the holy Ve:das
manju + prana:dam	= the repositories of divine melody
a. pa:litha:na:m	= protected
thvaya: + e:va	= only by you
kalpa + anthara	= during other eras
b. uchitha:na:m	= which are fit
alankarana	= to be adorned
kinkara	= by the devotees
thwath	= of yours

Oh Protector of the Holy Ve:das, Lord Hayagri:va! The diamond studded anklets of Your holy feet with their melodious sounds, are the casket of those Ve:das, which were regained by You in the form of Mathsya:vatha:ra, the Divine Fish and Hamsa:-vatha:ra, the Divine Swan, in times of yore. Those anklets are the repository of divine melody. Those divine feet with anklets, bless Your devotees, who adorn them on their heads out of devotion.

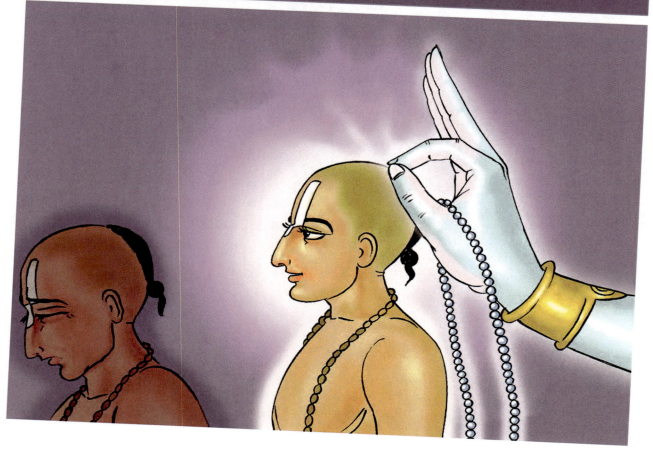

Chant this slo:ka to increase your retention power.

sanchinthaya:mi prathibha: das**a:sttha:n
sandhukshayantham samaya pradi:pa:n |
vijna:na kalpadruma pallava:bham
vya:khya:namudra: madhuram karam the: ||**   23

	sanchinthaya:mi	= I ruminate
	the:	= your
	karam	= divine hand
	vyakhya:na + mudra + madhuram	
	madhuram	= attractive
	vya:khya:na + mudra	= in a preaching seal (mudra:)
1.	vijna:na + kalpadruma + pallava + a:bham	
	a:bham	= the glow of which
	pallava	= is like the sprouting tender leaves
	kalpadruma	= of Kalpa Vruksha, a wish fulfilling tree
	vijna:na	= called Knowledge
2.	sandhukshayantham	= escalating
	pradi:pa:n	= the great lamps
	samaya	= called the doctrines
3.	prathibha + dasa: + sttha:n	
	sttha:n	= which are holding
	dasa:	= a wick
	prathibha	= called innovative knowledge

Lord Hayagri:va! I always meditate upon Your divine hand, which shines in a preaching and interpretative sign or seal, a feast to the eyes! You grant us immense powers of speech with all compassion. Our hearts, which hold the wick of knowledge like the earthen lamps, emit the luminous light called the doctrines. But these earthen lamps need the succor of oil. It should be proper and sufficient in quantity - neither high nor low! These lamps, our hearts need to be taken care of. Your affectionate blessing provides us with that support, without which, the wick loses its strength and the light fades out. Your grace provides that aid to the wick of innovative knowledge, and it engenders the light of the lamps of different sciences and doctrines.

It shines with the glow of the tender sprouts of the eternal tree of knowledge called Kalpa Vruksha. Moreover, Your divine hand itself is the Kalpa Vruksha and it has the sign of interpretative knowledge! Kalpa Vruksha can fulfill only some of our needs; but Your divine hand with its preaching and interpretative seal, fulfills all our needs and blesses us with salvation! I meditate on such sacred hand of Yours for developing retention and a great interpretative power.

Chant this slo:ka for sharp memory power.

chiththe: karo:mi sphuritha:ksha ma:lam
savye:tharam na:ttha! karam thwadi:yam |
jna:na:mrutho:danchana la:lasa:na:m
li:la:ghati: yanthra miva:sritha:na:m ||

24

na:ttha	= Oh Lord Hayagri:va!
karo:mi	= I hold
thwadi:yam	= your
savya + itharam	= right (other than the left)
karam	= hand
chiththe:	= in my heart
sphuritha + aksha + ma:lam	
sphuritha	= shining
aksha + ma:lam	= with a garland of beads
stthitham	= which stays
a:sritha:na:m	= to the surrendered
la:lasa:na:m	= having passion
udanchana	= to grab
amrutha	= nectar
jna:na	= of knowledge
iva	= like
ghati:yanthram	= an irrigation wheel
li:la:	= that moves effortlessly
prathibha	= called innovative knowledge

Lord Hayagri:va! I meditate on Your divine right hand in my heart forever. It always shines with a garland of chanting beads. It moves effortlessly like the irrigation wheel bringing out the nectar of knowledge for Your passionate devotees. I meditate on it for gaining the right knowledge.

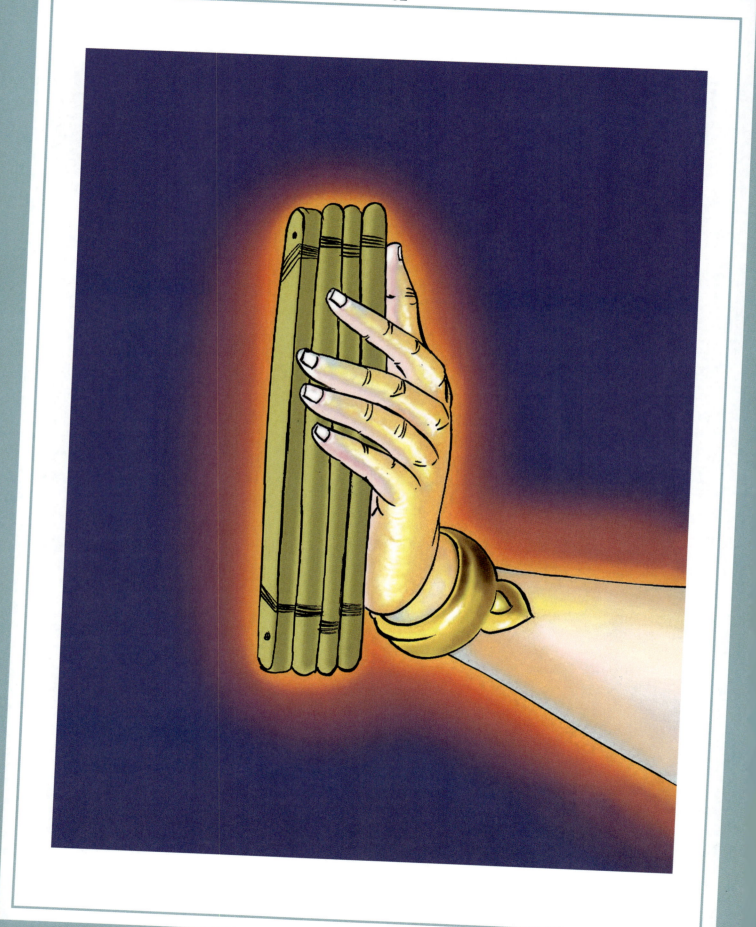

**prabo:dhasindho:r arunai:h praka:saihi
prava:la sangha:tha mivo:dvahantham |
vibha:vaye: de:va! sapusthakam the:
va:mam karam dakshinam a:sritha:na:m ||** 25

De:va	= Oh divine lord!
vibha:vaye:	= I sincerely assume
the:	= your
va:mam	= left
karam	= hand
arunai:hi	= shining with pinky
praka:saihi	= rays
a. sapusthakam	= holding scriptures
dakshinam	= capable of giving anything
a:sritha:na:m	= to the devotees
b. sthitham	= existing,
iva	= like
prava:la + sangha:tham	= a cluster of rubies
udwahantham	= brought out
prabo:dha + sindho:ho	= from the ocean of knowledge
li:la:	= that moves effortlessly
prathibha	= called innovative knowledge

Lord Hayagri:va! I worship Your left hand, which shines with a rosy hue. It appears to have been holding a heap of corals from the ocean of knowledge. It also holds a book of scriptures. It is capable of blessing the devotees with any kind of knowledge they want. I meditate on Your left hand for proper knowledge and wish fulfillment.

**thama:msi bhithva: visadair mayu:khaihi
sampri:nayantham vidushas chako:ra:n |
nisa:maye: thwa:m nava pundari:ke:
saradghane: chandram iva sphurantham ||** 26

nisa:maye:	= I serve
thwa:m	= You, the Lord
navapundari:ke:	= seated in the blossoming lotus
sphurantham	= shining
iva	= like
chandram	= the moon
ghane:	= amidst white clouds
sarath	= during autumn
a. sampri:nayantham	= who delights
chako:ra:n	= chako:ra: birds
vidushaha	= called scholars
b. bhithwa:	= and who pierces
thama:msi	= the inner darkness of ignorance
visadai:hi	= with pure
mayu:khai:hi	= graceful rays
prathibha	= called innovative knowledge

Lord Hayagri:va! You drive away the darkness of ignorance with the pure light of knowledge and You make the scholars happy. They all await Your divine light like the chako:ra: birds, which live only on moonlight as food. The scholars also await Your grace, which is their manna of knowledge. When you are seated on a newly blossomed lotus flower, You enchant us like the full moon on the autumnal clouds. I bow to You and serve You forever!

Chant this slo:ka for eloquent and endearing speech.

**disanthu me: de:va! sada: thwadi:ya:ha
daya:tharanga:nu chara:h kata:ksha:ha |
sro:thre:shu pumsa:m amrutham ksharanthi:m
saraswathi:m samsritha ka:madhe:num ||**   27

de:va		= Oh divine Lord!
sada:		= always
disanthu		= grant
me:		= me
thwadi:ya:ha		= your
kata:ksha:ha		= eternal glance
a.	daya: + tharanga + anuchara:ha	
	anuchara:ha	= which follow
	tharanga:ha	= the waves
	daya:	= of compassion
b.	saraswathi:m	= the flow of words
	ksharanthi:m	= which is like sprinkling
	amrutham	= the nectar
	srothre:shu	= in the ears
	pumsa:m	= of audience
c.	samsritha + ka:madhe:num	
	ka:madhe:num	= let it become Ka:madhe:nu, the wish fulfilling cow in the heaven
	samsritha	= for the approached

Oh radiant embodiment of the Light of Knowledge, Lord Hayagri:va! I request You to keep me in the shower of your benign sight with its tides of compassion. Bless me with the eloquent power of fluency and enable me to pour ambrosial words in the ears of the listeners. Bless me with the great power of eloquence like that of *Ka:madhe:nu*, the great divine cow, fulfilling the needs of those that approach with a desire. Lord Hayagri:va! Bless me with great qualities of speech!

Chant this slo:ka for victory in debates.

vi**s**e:shavith pa:rishade:shu na:ttha
vidagdha go:sh**tti**: samara:nga**n**e:shu |
jigi:shatho: me: kavitha:rki ke:ndra:n
jihva:gra simha:sanam abhyupe:ya:ha || 28

Na:ttha	= Oh Lord!
abhyupe:yaha	= please occupy
jihva: + agra + simha:sanam	
simha:sanam	= the throne
agra	= the top
jihva:	= of tongue
me:	= of mine
jigi:shathaha	= who wish to conquer
kavi + tha:rkika + indra:n -	
indra:n	= the greatest
kavi	= among poets and
tha:rkika	= among logicians
samara + angane:shu	= in the battlefields
vidagdha + go:shtti	= called intellectual competitions
vise:shavith + pa:rishade:shu -	
vise:sha + vith	= where wise & unbiased judges
pa:rishade:shu	= are present among the audience
ka:madhe:num	= let it become Ka:madhe:nu, the wish fulfilling cow in the heaven
samsritha	= for the approached

    Lord Hayagri:va! I wish to argue and conquer the best among the poets and the masters of logic and critical thinking. But such scholars must be well versed and proficient in all doctrines. The assembly of proficient scholars should be like great battle fields. It must have wise and erudite scholars who would be able to judge the winners with impartiality. Hence, when I participate and argue in such conferences, I pray to You to make my tongue as your throne. Bless me with great eloquence and victory over such poet laureates and masters of logic!

Chant this slo:ka to win the debates.

thwa:m chinthayan thvanmayatha:m prapannaha
thwa:mudgru**n**an **s**abdamaye:na dha:mna: |
swa:min sama:je:shu same:dhishi:ya
swachhanda va:da:hava baddha**s**u:raha || 29

Swa:min	= Oh Lord!
same:dhishi:ya	= let me be glorified
sama:je:shu	= during debates
baddha + su:raha	= by cornering the scholars
swachhanda	= who instigate illogically
a:hava	= in the war
va:da	= of arguments
prapannaha	= after attaining
thwanmayatha:m	= equality with you
chinthayan	= by remembering
thwa:m	= you
uth + grunan	= and establishing
thwa:m	= you
dha:mna	= through Ve:dic mass
sabdamaye:na	= which is the repository of manthras
ka:madhe:num	= let it become Ka:madhe:nu, the wish fulfilling cow in the heaven
samsritha	= for the approached

Lord Hayagri:va! You are the glorious embodiment of all the Sacred Manthras and Knowledge. I meditate on You, singing your praise. Let me realize Your divine presence in my heart always. I want to grow and get glorified in the intellectual assemblies by defeating great warriors called scholars who try to instigate illogical arguments. I pray to bless me with all the great powers of debating skills and fulfill my desire to defeat all the experts of debate during intellectual assemblies.

na:na: vidha:na:m agathih kala:na:m
nacha:pi thi:rtthe:shu krutha:vatha:raha |
dhruvam thawa:na:ttha parigraha:ya:ha
navam navam pa:thram aham daya:ya:ha || 30

agathihi	= I'm bereft
na:na:vidha:na:m	= of many kinds
kala:na:m	= of scriptures
na + cha	= neither did I
krutha + avatha:raha	= bow down
thi:rtthe:shu	= at the feet of great Gurus
api	= in spite of that
aham	= I am
navam + navam	= afresh and uniquely
pa:thram	= qualified
daya:ya:ha	= for the compassion
thava	= of yours
ana:ttha + parigraha:ya	
parigraha:ya	= which accepts
ana:ttha	= even the abandoned
dhruvam	= this is certain
samsritha	= for the approached

Lord Hayagri:va! I am an ignoramus. I am bereft of intellectual wealth. I did not serve my Gurus enough, who were masters of Scriptures. I have no other savior but You, thesource of ultimate knowledge. Let me be in Your good grace. Drench me with Your incessant compassion!

**akampani:ya: nyapani:thi bhe:daihi
alankrushi:ran hrudayam madi:yam |
sanka: kalanka:paga mo:jjwala:ni
thaththwa:ni samyanchi thawa prasa:da:th || 31**

samyanchi	= Let the eternal
thathwa:ni	= concepts
1. sanka: + kalanka + apagama + ujjwala:ni	
ujjwala:ni	= which are vibrant
apagama	= after elimination
sanka: + kalanka	= of doubts and misinterpretations
2. akampani:ya:ni	= unshakable
apani:thi + bhe:daihi	= by any kind of irrational arguments
alankrushi:ran	= beautify
madi:yam	= my
hrudayam	= mind
prasa:da:th	= by the grace
thava	= of yours
samsritha	= for the approached

Oh Lord Hayagri:va! You have blessed me with the knowledge of all the three realities, The Supreme Soul Na:ra:yana, Innumerable Souls and The Mysterious Nature. My knowledge is unshakable by Your Divine Grace. Let my mind remain doubt free and be always decorated with the pure knowledge of these ultimate truths.

**vya:khya: mudra:m kara sarasijaih pusthakam sankha chakre:
bibhrad bhinna sphatika ruchire: pundari:ke: nishannaha |
amla:na sri:r amrutha visadair amsubhih pla:vayanma:m
a:virbhu:ya:d anagha mahima: ma:nase: va:gadhi:saha || 32**

  va:k + adhi:saha   = Let the Lord of knowledge
 a. anagha + mahima: = whose greatness has no limit
 b. amla:na + sri:hi
   ` sri:hi   = whose blossom
   amla:na   = never withers
 c. nishannaha   = who dwells
   pundari:ke: = in a white lotus
   bhinna + sphatika + ruchire:
   ruchire: = that glows
   bhinna + sphatika = like a broken crystal
   bibhrath   = holding
 1. vya:khya: + mudra:m = the seal of preaching
 2. sankha + chakre: = the divine conch and disc
 3. pusthakam   = the holy scriptures
 4. kara + sarasijai:hi = with lotus like hands
  a:virbhu:ya:th   = emerge
  ma:nase: = in the heart
  mama   = of mine
  pla:vayan   = soaking
  ma:m   = me
  amrutha + visadai:hi = with pure and eternal
  amsubhihi   = rays of grace
  mama   = of mine
  pla:vayan   = soaking
  ma:m   = me
  amrutha + visadai:hi = with pure and eternal

May the glorious form of Hayagri:va emerge in my heart! His form is a great feast to my eyes. He shines with four lotus like hands with the divine conch and disc, scriptures and Jna:na Mudra, the seal of preaching. He shines with the brightness of a splintered crystal gem on a white lotus flower. His never fading radiance has an immense power. I pray to such Lord Hayagri:va, the Ocean of Divine Attributes, to appear in my heart and drench me with the eternal and benign rays of immaculate piety.

va:garttha siddhi he:tho:h pa**tt**atha
hayagri:va samsthuthim bhakthya: |
kavitha:rkika ke:sari**n**a:
ve:nkatana:tthe:na virachitha:m e:tha:m || 33

pattatha	= please read
bhakthya:	= with devotion
e:tha:m	= this
Hayagri:va + samsthuthim	
samsthuthim	= eulogy
hayagri:va	= on Lord Hayagri:va
a. virachitha:m	= which were written
ve:nkatana:tthe:na	= by Sri Venkatana:ttha
b. kavi + tha:rkika + ke:sarina:	= whose title is 'kavi tha:rkikake:sari:'
va:k + arttha + siddhi + he:tho:ho	
he:tho:ho	= to attain
siddhi	= mastery
va:k	= on words
arttha	= and their meaning
samsubhihi	= rays of grace
mama	= of mine
pla:vayan	= soaking
ma:m	= me
amrutha + visadai:hi	= with pure and eternal

This stho:thra was written on Lord Hayagri:va by Swamy Ve:da:ntha De:sika, whose original name was Sri Ve:nkata Na:ttha:cha:rya. His title was *Kavitha:rkika Ke:sari:* (the Lion among the poets and critical thinkers). Learn this stho:thram with devotion for a great eloquence and mastery over words and their meanings for a perfect and powerful speech.

kavitha:rkika simha:ya kalya:na gunasa:line: |
sri:mathe: ve:nkate:sa:ya ve:da:ntha gurave: namaha ||

Sri: Hayagri:va Mangala:sasanam

sarva vidya: swaru:pa:ya lakshmi: samslishta vakshase: |
madupa:sana lakshya:ya hayagri:va:ya mangalam ||

sri: hayagri:va parabramhane: namaha
Jai Sri:manna:ra:yana!!

Made in the USA
Middletown, DE
23 August 2024

59596949R00046